A BIT OF EVERYTHING

(Un Peu De Tout)

Games, Activities, and Cue Cards for Introducing French to Young Children

Written and Illustrated
Liza Sernett

Publishers
T.S. Denison and Company, Inc.
Minneapolis, Minnesota 55431

T.S. Denison & Co., Inc.

"Materials designed by teachers, for teachers" is a statement that the T.S. Denison Company is extremely proud of. All of our quality educational products are tried, tested, and proven effective—by teachers!

For over 100 years, T.S. Denison has been a leader in educational publishing. Thousands of teachers look to us for new and innovative aids to make their work more enjoyable and more rewarding. We are committed to developing and publishing educational materials that will assist teachers in building a strong curriculum for young children.

Plan for great teaching experiences when you use materials from the T.S. Denison Company.

Dedication

I dedicate this book to all the children at *Starting Space*.
Thank you for teaching me the importance of savoring
one's creativity, sense of humor, and desire to learn!

Standard Book Number: 0-513-02064-0
A Bit of Everything French (Un Peu De Tout)
Copyright © 1991 by T.S. Denison & Co., Inc.
Minneapolis, Minnesota 55431

Printed in the USA

INTRODUCTION

This book is designed for any teacher who has a desire to introduce his/her students to the French language in a fun and exciting way. Neither the teacher nor the students need to have any previous language experience. Pronunciations are given clearly and adapted easily.

The book is broken down into 13 different units of study. Each unit begins with an English/French vocabulary list that will introduce the teacher to the vocabulary that will be taught within that unit. Each unit concludes with cue cards that are printed with the French vocabulary on one side and the English translation on the reverse. These cards can be cut out and put into an index file for quick reference.

In each of the units you will also find Fun Sheets. These sheets are to provide the students with a miniature study book of their own. The sheets should be saved until all the units are completed and then made into a book that the students can share with others or review for themselves.

By using a hands-on, experiential approach for introducing a foreign language, young children will quickly begin using their "new" vocabulary words in their day to day activities.

Table of Contents

UNIT 1

DAYS OF THE WEEK

VOCABULARY

		(pronunciation)
Monday	lundi	*luhn-dee*
Tuesday	mardi	*mahr-dee*
Wednesday	mercredi	*mehr-kruh-dee*
Thursday	jeudi	*zhuh-dee*
Friday	vendredi	*von-druh-dee*
Saturday	samedi	*sahm-dee*
Sunday	dimanche	*dee-mahnsh*

DAYS OF THE WEEK

Incorporating the French translation of the days of the week into your regular curriculum can be done many ways. One very simple method is to alter your room calendar slightly. By attaching cue cards with the French words for the appropriate day of the week, children find a new dimension to the classroom calendar. As children become familiar with the new French vocabulary, encourage them to recite the words before revealing the cue card's English equivalent.

CALENDAR GAMES

Games are another enjoyable way to integrate the French days of the week into the curriculum. Collect some cardboard pieces and using a permanent marker write down the new French vocabulary. Punch holes into either ends of the cardboard and attach a string through the holes; this makes it possible for children to wear the word. Divide the class into groups of eight children. Have seven of the children wear the seven French days of the week. The remaining child must try to align the children in the correct order and then recite (in French) the days of the week. For added fun, have relays or timed races. This game is recommended for children who already have a fairly developed understanding of the new vocabulary.

SONGS TO REINFORCE

Any music already existing with English lyrics can be used by replacing with the new French vocabulary. Children can make patterns of beats for the days of the week as well. Let one child clap the beats of the syllables in the word "lundi." Then let the next child clap the syllables in the word "mardi." Continue the process until every child has had a chance to clap the beats of at least one day of the week. This way all of the children have experienced the pronunciation of the new vocabulary words in slow repetition.

DAYS OF THE WEEK
FUN SHEET

Using the space provided in the right hand column, draw a picture of the things that you would like to do on any given day of the week. The left column indicates the day that you would participate in that activity. Be prepared to share your ideas with your friends using the new French vocabulary for the days of the week.

LUNDI	
MARDI	
MERCREDI	
JEUDI	
VENDREDI	
SAMEDI	
DIMANCHE	

Unit 1 Vocabulary – Days of the Week

lundi	**mardi**
mercredi	**jeudi**
vendredi	**samedi**
dimanche	

Unit 1 Vocabulary – Days of the Week

Tuesday	**Monday**
Thursday	**Wednesday**
Saturday	**Friday**
	Sunday

UNIT 2

MONTHS OF THE YEAR

VOCABULARY

		(pronunciation)
January	janvier	*zhawnv-yay*
February	février	*fayv-ree-ay*
March	mars	*mahrss*
April	avril	*a-vreel*
May	mai	*meh*
June	juin	*zhwan*
July	juillet	*zhwee-yay*
August	août	*oot*
September	septembre	*sehp-tawmbr*
October	octobre	*ohk-toh-bruh*
November	novembre	*noh-vawmbr*
December	décembre	*day-sawmbr*
Autumn	l'automne	*loh-tohn*
Winter	l'hiver	*lee-vehr*
Spring	le printemps	*luh pran-tahn*
Summer	l'été	*lay-tay*

BIRTHDAY GAME

MONTHS OF THE YEAR CALENDAR

Like the vocabulary for the days of the week, the new French vocabulary for the months of the year can also be integrated into your regular curriculum. Using two loose-leaf book rings, construct your own "rolodex" of cue cards containing the spelling and pronunciation of all twelve months in English and French. Place this rolodex near the room calendar and use it for recitation and for the game described below. Laminating the cue cards will preserve them for future years.

If you keep a birthday calendar in your room, add some French flavor by playing the Birthday Game. Children love celebrating their special day of the year. Have them tell you their birth month using the new French vocabulary in this unit. If you have children who may be too young to recall the month they were born, come prepared to class with those dates. Begin by reciting the months of the year in French slowly. When the children hear their month they stand until the next month is introduced. Pick up speed as you go through the months a second and third time. Children love the movement and speed so be prepared for some volume! Variations might include having the children clap, sit, or if you are really brave, have them shout back the month when it is called.

SEASONS

Divide the class of children into four equal groups. Set up work stations in four different areas of your classroom. Assign each group to a work station. Explain to the children that each work station represents one of the four seasons. Label each "seasonal" station with the french name for that season.

Send the groups to their particular seasonal station. At their station the children should discuss the activities and weather conditions that are special to that season. Upon completion of the discussion the children, (as a group) should paint a picture of their assigned season. When the seasonal picture is completed, each group will have the opportunity to present their seasonal picture to the rest of the class.

Have each of the children use the following sentence to begin their description of their painting and tell about the activities of that season that they like.

Dans l'été
(dahn) **l'hiver**
l'automne
le printemps

j'aime _____.
I like
(zh'ehm)

(In the season I like _____.)

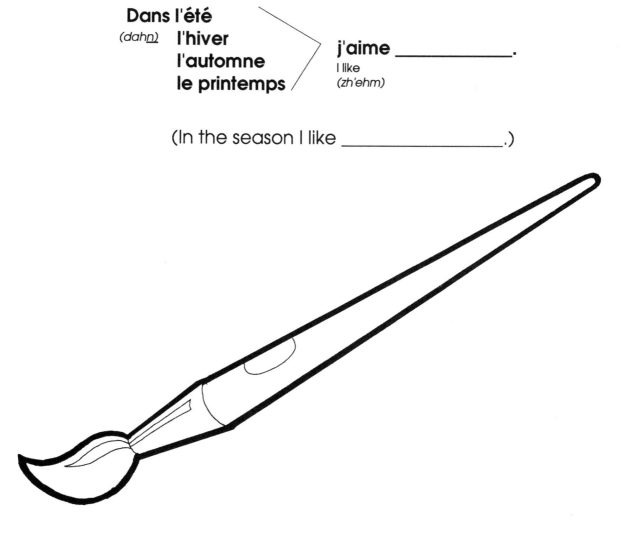

Cut out the pictures and glue them next to the month that best matches that picture.

janvier	**juillet**
février	**août**
mars	**septembre**
avril	**octobre**
mai	**novembre**
juin	**décembre**

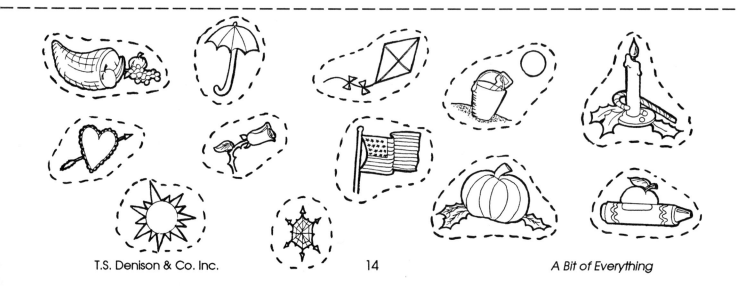

Unit 2 Vocabulary – Months of the Year

janvier	février
mars	avril
mai	juin
juillet	août
septembre	octobre

Unit 2 Vocabulary – Months of the Year

February	**January**
April	**March**
June	**May**
August	**July**
October	**September**

novembre	décembre
l'automne	l'hiver
le printemps	l'été

Unit 2 Vocabulary – Months of the Year

December

November

Winter

Autumn

Summer

Spring

UNIT 3

NUMBERS

3 4 5 1 2 8

VOCABULARY

		(pronunciation)
one	un	*uhn*
two	deux	*duh*
three	trois	*trwah*
four	quatre	*kah-truh*
five	cinq	*sank*
six	six	*seess*
seven	sept	*seht*
eight	huit	*weet*
nine	neuf	*nuhf*
ten	dix	*deess*
eleven	onze	*ohnz*
twelve	douze	*dooz*
thirteen	treize	*trehz*
fourteen	quatorze	*kah-tohrz*
fifteen	quinze	*kanz*
sixteen	seize	*sehz*
seventeen	dix-sept	*dee-seht*
eighteeen	dix-huit	*deez-weet*
nineteen	dix-neuf	*deez-nuhf*
twenty	vingt	*van*

NUMBERS
CALENDAR

Using your room calendar, you can teach the days of the week, the months of the year and numbers in French. Children love some change in the regularity of routine. Having the children recite the numbers leading to the actual date in French can be fun. For some variety, read the numbers backwards or have a child lead the recitation. You could give a title to the child leading the recitation: "Mademoiselle/Monsieur Numero" (Miss/Mister Number).

NUMBER BINGO

Copy the four cards provided on the following pages so that each child in the class has at least one card. Then use paint or magic marker to label nine ping pong balls or pieces of paper with numbers 1 to 9. Use whatever you can think of for the children to mark off the numbers on their card (dots, beans, popcorn kernels, etc.). Put the squares or balls in a concealed container and proceed with the regular game of Bingo. In this game however, you can only use numbers in French. Pick different children to be the number caller.

NUMBER BINGO

1	3	4
5	9	7
8	2	6

NUMBER BINGO

8	1	5
3	6	4
9	2	7

NUMBER BINGO

8	6	3
2	4	7
9	5	1

NUMBER BINGO

9	3	6
2	5	7
4	1	8

FROG HOP GAME

This game requires advanced planning. Cut out 10 large green lily pads from felt or construction paper. With a marker or felt put a single number from 1 to 10 on each lily pad. Use the pattern included to make a frog costume. For durability felt is recommended, but paper is fine.

When lily pads and the costume are prepared you can begin the game. Have one child dress up as the frog. Tape the lily pads around the room 1 to 1 1/2 feet apart. Then instruct the child dressed as the frog to jump from lily pad to lily pad giving out the number indicated on the lily pad as he/she jumps. The number must be given in French. For variation, have the frog jump and the other children shout out the numbers that the frog is jumping on. This game encourages learning through excitement and movement.

(Make 2)

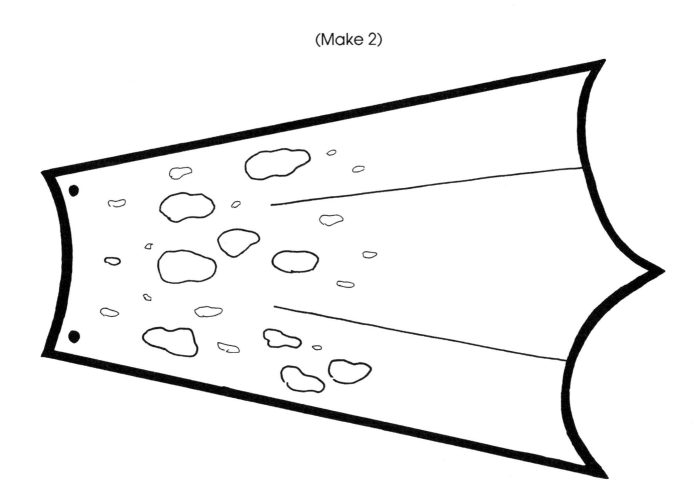

(Punch holes and add string so frog feet can be worn by the children)

FROG HOP GAME

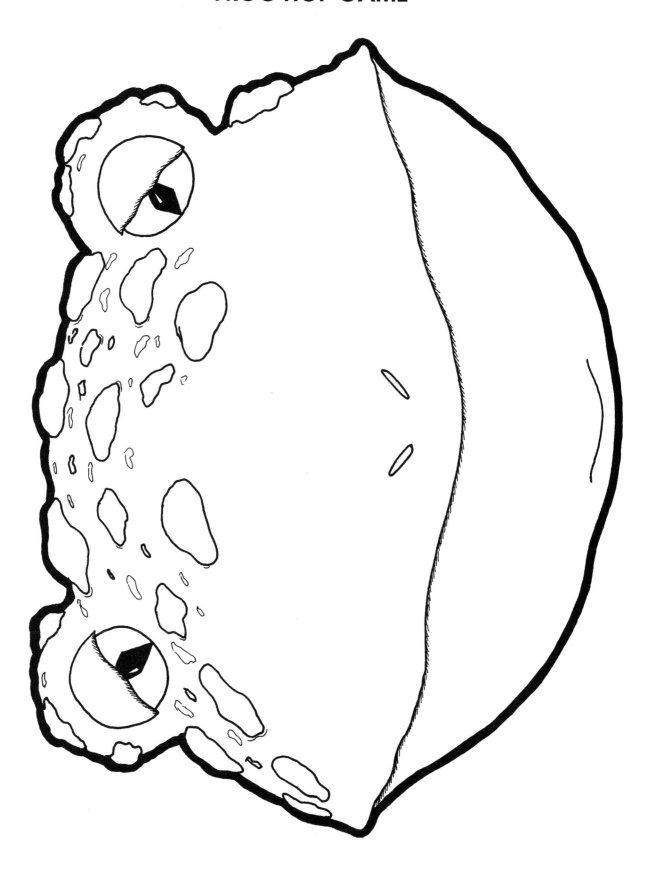

(Punch holes and add string so the frog face can be worn as a mask.)

FROG HOP GAME

THE NUMBER GAME

Copy pages 26 and 27 to create the numbers gameboard. *To begin the game:* give each child a penny to use as a marker on the gameboard. The children take turns rolling the dice. The player with the highest number on the dice goes first. *To play the game:* The children take turns rolling the dice and then moving that number of spaces on the gameboard. The children should be encouraged to say the numbers in French. The player who reaches the finish line first is the winner.

START

FINISH

MAIL BOX GAME

Collect 10 shoe boxes before beginning this game. Wrap the boxes with butcher paper carefully so that the lids are removable. Then label them from 1 to 10. Make a slit (the size of a letter envelope) in the top of each box. Attach a flag (made out of construction paper) with a brad to each box. Then label 10 letter envelopes with the numbers 1 to 10. When this is all complete you are ready to begin the game.

Place the mail boxes around the room so their numbers are clearly visible. Appoint a child to be the mail deliverer. If you can find a mail bag or large purse the game is even more interesting. Put the letters in the bag. Without peeking, have the mail person choose a letter from the bag. Then he/she must hold the letter envelope up so that all the children can give the matching French mail box number. The child must then deliver the letter to the correct mailbox. Try moving the mail boxes around the room every few days.

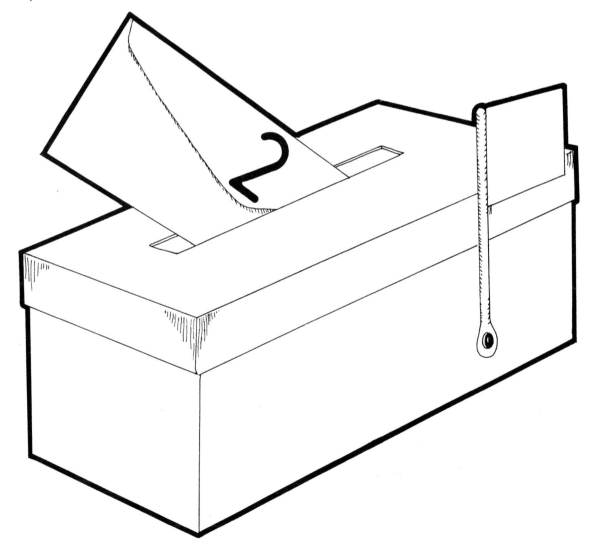

un	deux
trois	quatre
cinq	six
sept	huit
neuf	dix

2 two	1 one
4 four	3 three
6 six	5 five
8 eight	7 seven
10 ten	9 nine

onze	douze
treize	quatorze
quinze	seize
dix-sept	dix-huit
dix-neuf	vingt

12 twelve	**11** eleven
14 fourteen	**13** thirteen
16 sixteen	**15** fifteen
18 eighteen	**17** seventeen
20 twenty	**19** nineteen

UNIT 4

COLORS

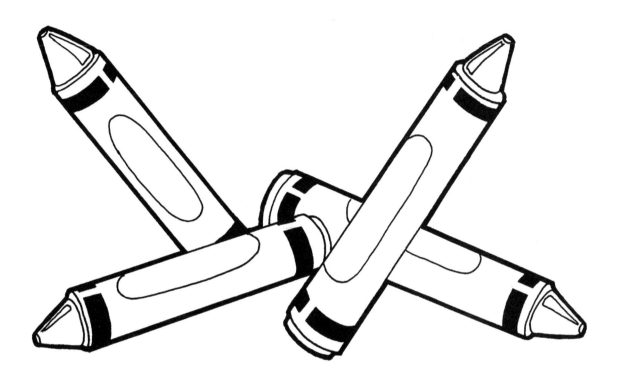

VOCABULARY

(pronunciation)

red	rouge	roozh
green	vert	vair
orange	orange	o-ronzh
yellow	jaune	zhohn
blue	bleu	bluh
purple	violet	veeh-o-lay
black	noir	nwahr
white	blanc	blōn
pink	rose	rohz
brown	brun	bruhn

COLOR BINGO

Copy the bingo cards on pages 34 to 36, producing enough copies for each child in the class to have at least one card. Have the children shade in the appropriate color in each square (use the vocabulary at the beginning of the unit for assistance). Color and cut out the 10 circles seen on page 37 and put them in a concealed container – these will be drawn to determine what corresponding square on the card may be covered up. Use dots, beans, popcorn kernels, etc., to mark the cards when the colors are called.

Have a student act as the color caller and instruct him/her to only use the French vocabulary words for the colors he/she draws from the container. Use regular Bingo rules (of 3 squares in a row) to determine the winner. The winner then should become the color caller.

COLOR BINGO		
ROUGE	NOIR	BLEU
ORANGE	JAUNE	VIOLET
VERT	BLANC	BRUN

COLOR BINGO

ROUGE	NOIR	JAUNE
BLANC	BRUN	ORANGE
BLEU	VERT	ROSE

COLOR BINGO

NOIR	BLEU	ORANGE
JAUNE	BRUN	VERT
BLANC	VIOLET	ROUGE

COLOR BINGO

VERT	VIOLET	BRUN
ORANGE	BLANC	NOIR
JAUNE	BLEU	ROUGE

COLOR BINGO

BLEU	NOIR	JAUNE
BRUN	VIOLET	ROUGE
ROSE	VERT	ORANGE

COLOR BINGO

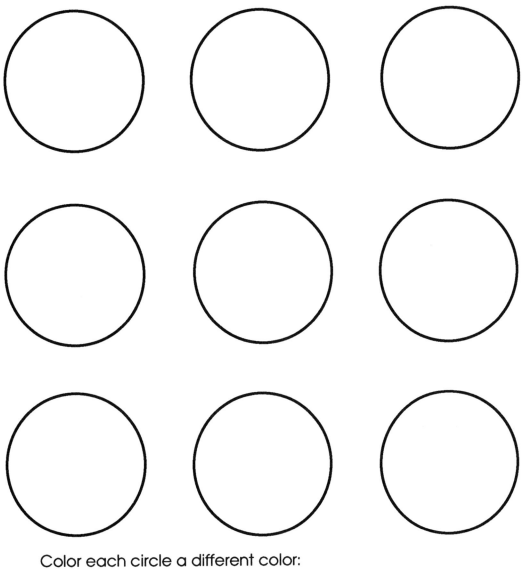

Color each circle a different color:

rouge
vert
orange
jaune
bleu
violet
noir
blanc
rose
brun

COLOR MATCHING GAME

Copy the pattern of the bear and shirt. Make eight copies. Color the eight bears' shorts different colors (blue, red, green, yellow, white, black, orange and purple). Color the shirts with matching colors. You may wish to laminate these items and encourage children to use the game during their free time.

To begin the game, select eight children and give them each a single bear. Have them leave the room and give eight other children a single shirt. Then invite the other children holding bears to re-enter the room. Those children holding the shirts should be concealing the color of the shirt from those children holding the bears. Those holding the bears must ask children in the room if they might have a particular color shirt that would match their bears' shorts. The key is to only use French vocabulary words for the colors. The child who finds the matching shirt for his bear must call out his color in French and sit down before the others have found their matches.

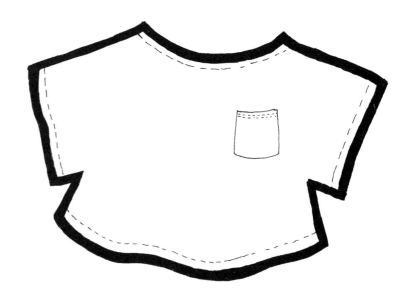

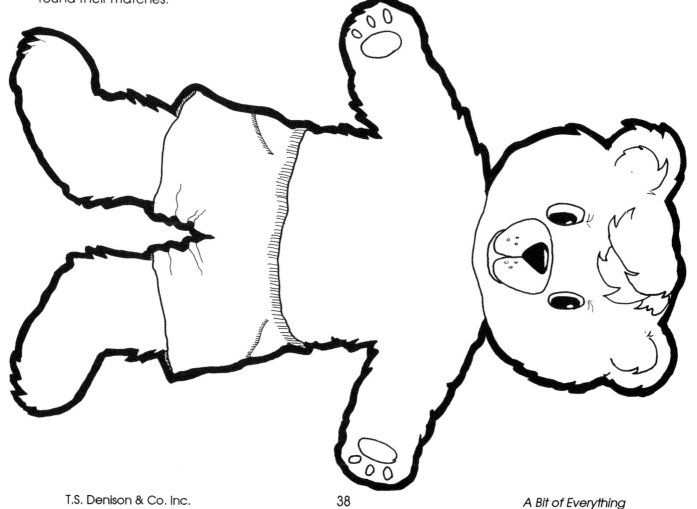

Below is a spin dial of colors with the French color vocabulary labeled. Copy and glue dial to a heavier cardboard. The spinner can also be copied and glued to a heavier paper. Using a brad, attach the spinner to the center point indicated on the dial. Allow children the chance to spin the dial and take turns naming the indicated color in French.

SPIN DIAL FOR COLORS

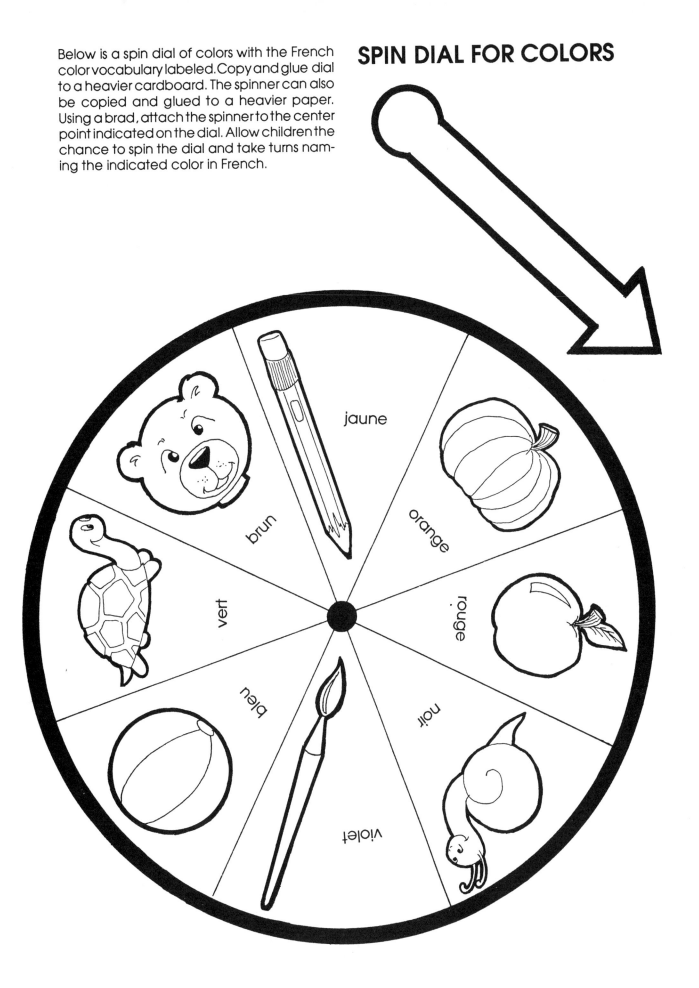

NAME _____

Draw a line from the colored crayon on the left to the object of the corresponding color on the right. Then, choose a friend and check each other's answers. Remember to use French vocabulary in your discussions.

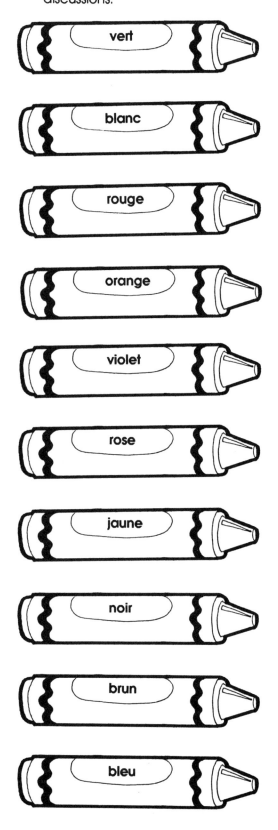

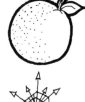

rouge	jaune
vert	bleu
orange	violet
blanc	noir
rose	brun

Unit 4 Vocabulary – Colors

yellow	**red**
blue	**green**
purple	**orange**
black	**white**
brown	**pink**

UNIT 5
WEATHER

VOCABULARY

It's sunny	Il fait du soleil	*(pronunciation)* *eel feh dew soh-laye*
It's hot	Il fait chaud	*eel feh shoh*
It's cloudy	Il fait gris	*eel feh gree*
It's cool (fresh)	Il fait frais	*eel feh freh*
It's raining	Il pleut	*eel pluh*
It's cold	Il fait froid	*eel feh frwah*
It's snowing	Il neige	*eel nehzh*
It's windy	Il fait du vent	*eel feh dew vahn*
It's bad, ugly out	Il fait mauvais	*eel feh moh-veh*
It's beautiful	Il fait beau	*eel feh boh*

WEATHER PATTERNS

Use the patterns below to cut felt shapes for various weather conditions. They can be used on a felt board or they could become a part of the room's decor. If left at an appropriate height in the room, children can use the patterns during their free time. Children must always employ their French vocabulary when using this material. These patterns can also be used for the *News Bulletin Game* described on the next page.

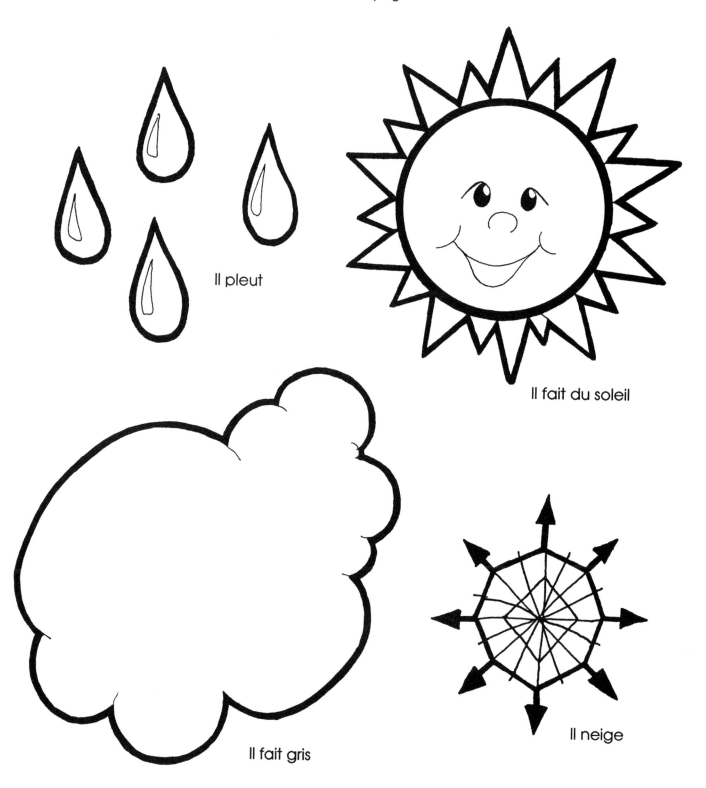

Il pleut

Il fait du soleil

Il fait gris

Il neige

NEWS BULLETIN FOR WEATHER

Keeping a daily weather bulletin in the classroom is helpful in strengthening French vocabulary in this area. Use a large piece of bristol board and write the following short sentences in large letters . . .

Today is _____ **, le** _____ _____ **,** _____ **.**
        day   *date*   *month*   *year*

The weather is _____ **.**
                        *what weather **looks** like*

The temperature is _____ **.**
                        *what weather **feels** like*

In the blank spots place the day of the week, the date, the month and the year. This can be done in French or English depending on the unit your are working on and the comprehension level of the children. Place the type of weather in the next blank. This can be done with French words or weather pattern cut-outs (see page 44). Be certain the children are using their new vocabulary terms to describe the day. The temperature blanks can be filled with any of the three main temperatures... Il fait frais, Il fait froid, or Il fait chaud. Doing this exercise everyday is enjoyable and the repetition will become part of long term memory storage. As the children progress with their French, have them fill all the blanks with French vocabulary.

Below are three thermometers. Each has a different French phrase below it telling how hot or cold it is outside. You can show the mercury levels in the thermometers by coloring them red to the correct levels.

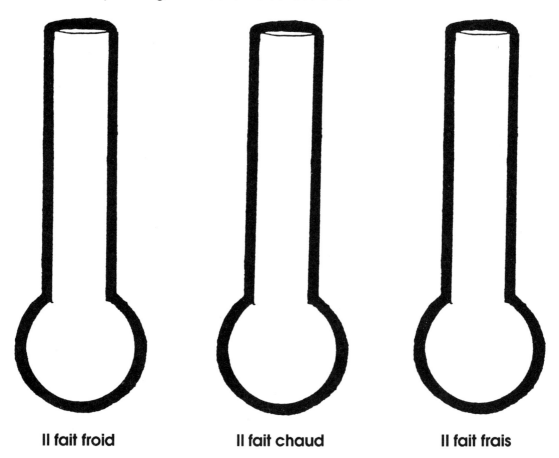

Il fait froid   **Il fait chaud**   **Il fait frais**

- -

Color the different weather patterns. Take some time to discuss the types of weather with your friend. Remember to use your new French vocabulary for weather and temperatures.

il fait du soleil	il fait chaud
il fait gris	il fait frais
il pleut	il fait froid
il neige	il fait du vent
il fait mauvais	il fait beau

Unit 5 Vocabulary – Weather

It's hot

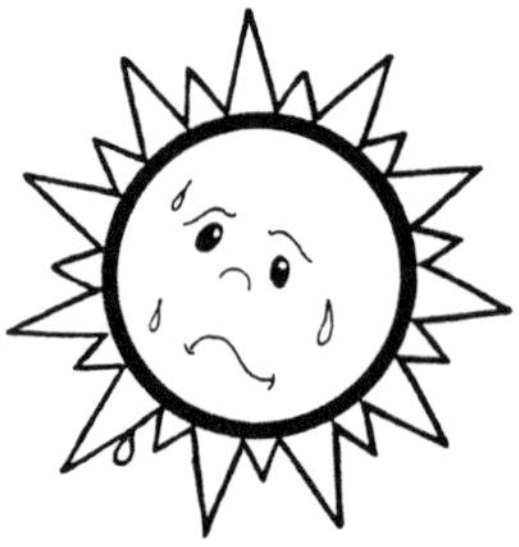

It's sunny

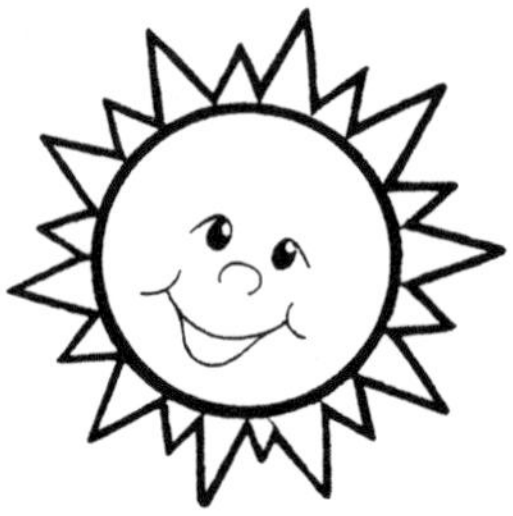

It's cool, just right

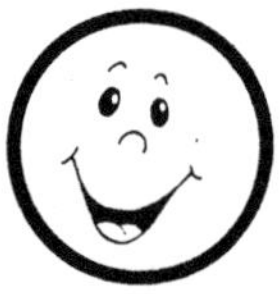

It's cloudy

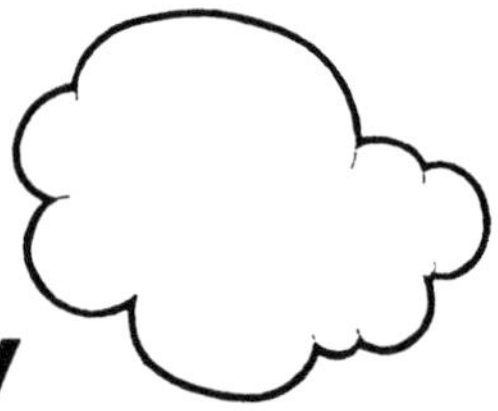

It's cold

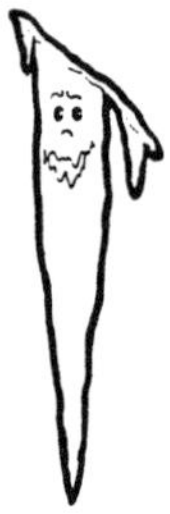

It's raining

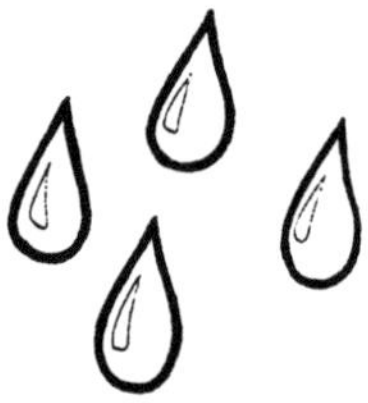

It's windy

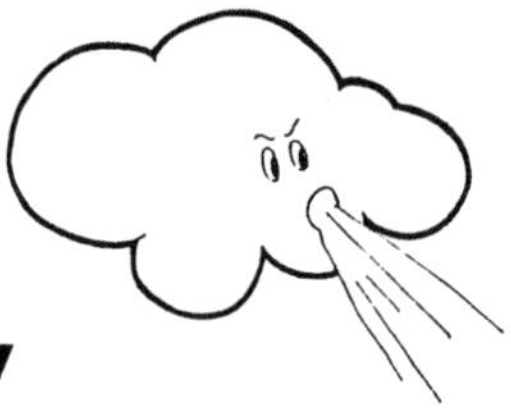

It's snowing

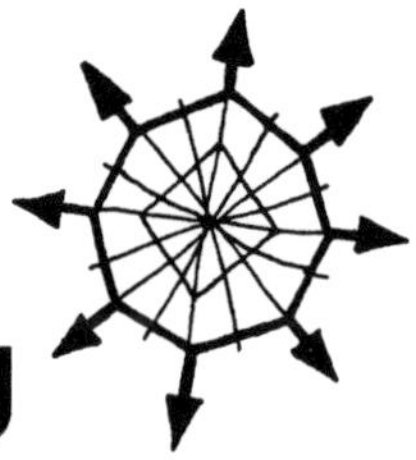

It's beautiful

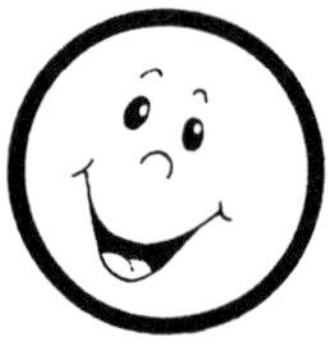

It's bad out

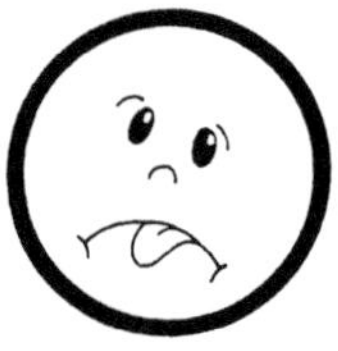

UNIT 6

PARTS
OF THE BODY

VOCABULARY

		(pronunciation)
ears	les oreilles	*layz oh-ray*
mouth	la bouche	*lah boosh*
nose	le nez	*luh nay*
eyes	les yeux	*layz yuh*
shoulders	les épaules	*layz ay-pohl*
arms	les bras	*lay brah*
hands	les mains	*lay ma<u>n</u>*
legs	les jambes	*lay zhawmb*
knees	les genoux	*lay zhuh-noo*
feet	les pieds	*lay p'yay*
hair	les cheveux	*lay shuh-vuh*

PARTS OF THE BODY

"Simon Dit" ("Simon Says") is a timeless game children love. Try using the French Body Parts vocabulary to play "Simon Dit" (Seemon Dee). Initially, as children are first getting acquainted with his/her own body parts, they will be watching and learning both visually and auditorally. Eventually advance to having the leader give the directions without any visual clues. Finally, take turns allowing children to play the role of Simon.

HEAD AND SHOULDERS, KNEES AND TOES SONG

"Head And Shoulders, Knees And Toes" is a song most children are familiar with. Start by singing the song slowly and gradually speed up the pace. Watch the children have a great time with this French variation of this old song.

TÊTE, ÉPAULES, GENOUX ET PIEDS

Tête, épaules, genoux et pieds,
      genoux et pieds. (répèté)
J'ai deux yeux, un nez, une bouche,
      et deux oreilles.
Tête, épaules, genoux et pieds,
      genoux et pieds.

MONSIEUR JAUNE – PARTS OF THE BODY

Monsieur Jaune (Mister Yellow) is easily adapted into any classroom environment. Not only do the children enjoy using him as a French learning tool during group times but he is also enjoyed during play time in which children use him in game formats.

Monsieur Jaune's objective is to teach children basic body parts in an enjoyable way. Using the cut-out patterns found on pages 53 to 55, Monsieur Jaune can be cut out of felt or construction paper. Have children take turns adding parts to his body and identifying each part in English and French until Monsieur Jaune's body is complete. *(Note: Monsieur Jaune's main body parts should be cut from yellow paper or felt to help reinforce the French colors. If cutting Monsieur Jaune from construction paper, laminating the parts is advised. This allows for greater child participation during free play and a greater longevity of Monsieur Jaune.)*

The body parts of Monsieur Jaune may be labeled on one side to help reinforce the new French terms as children are being introduced to this vocabulary. As they progress, try using the reverse side without any labels to construct Monsieur Jaune.

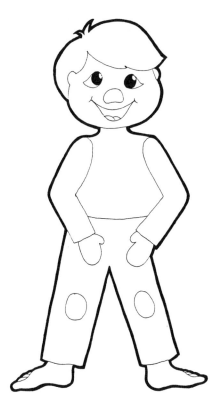

THE BODY PARTS OF "MONSIEUR JAUNE"

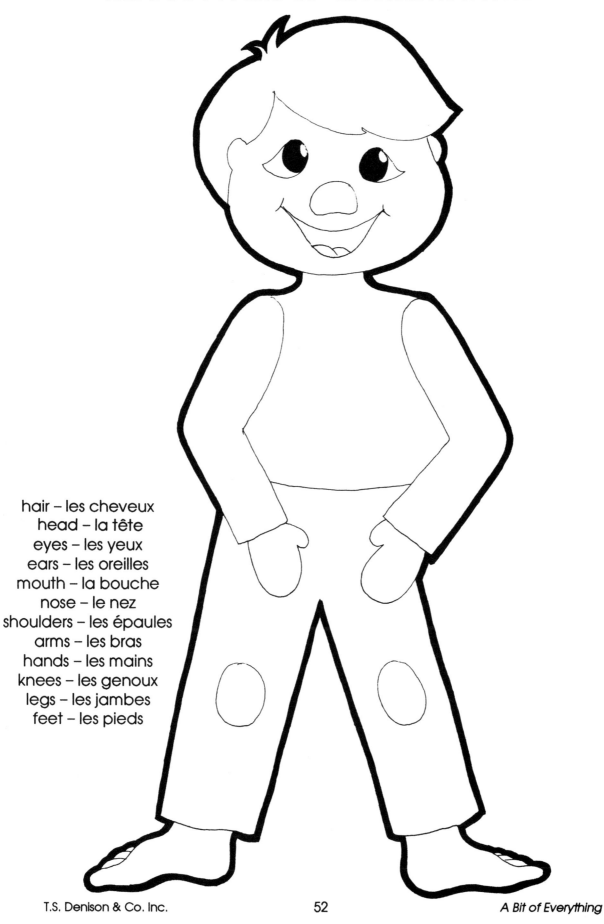

hair – les cheveux
head – la tête
eyes – les yeux
ears – les oreilles
mouth – la bouche
nose – le nez
shoulders – les épaules
arms – les bras
hands – les mains
knees – les genoux
legs – les jambes
feet – les pieds

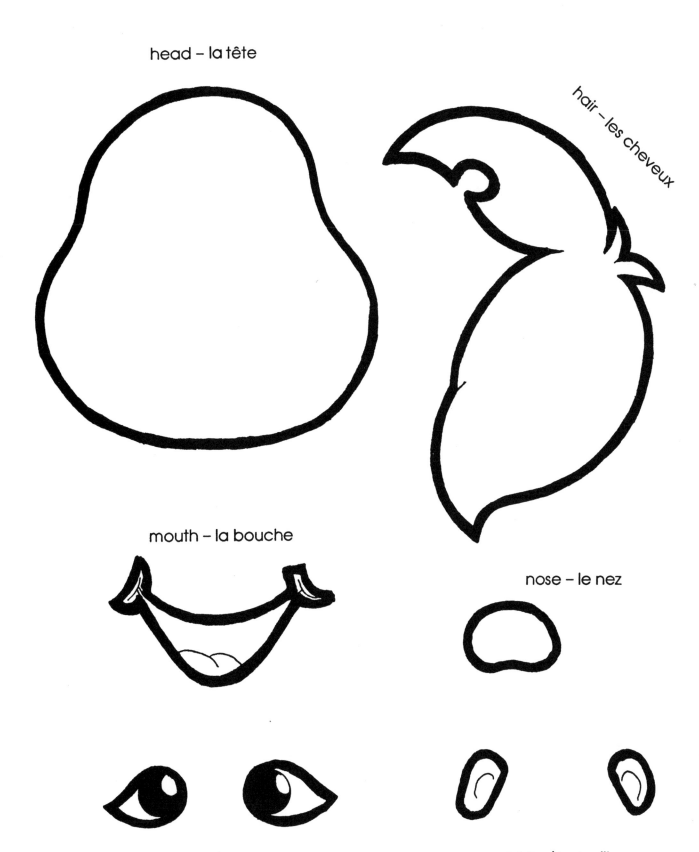

head – la tête

hair – les cheveux

mouth – la bouche

nose – le nez

eyes – les yeux

ears – les oreilles

MONSIEUR JAUNE PATTERNS

shoulders – les épaules

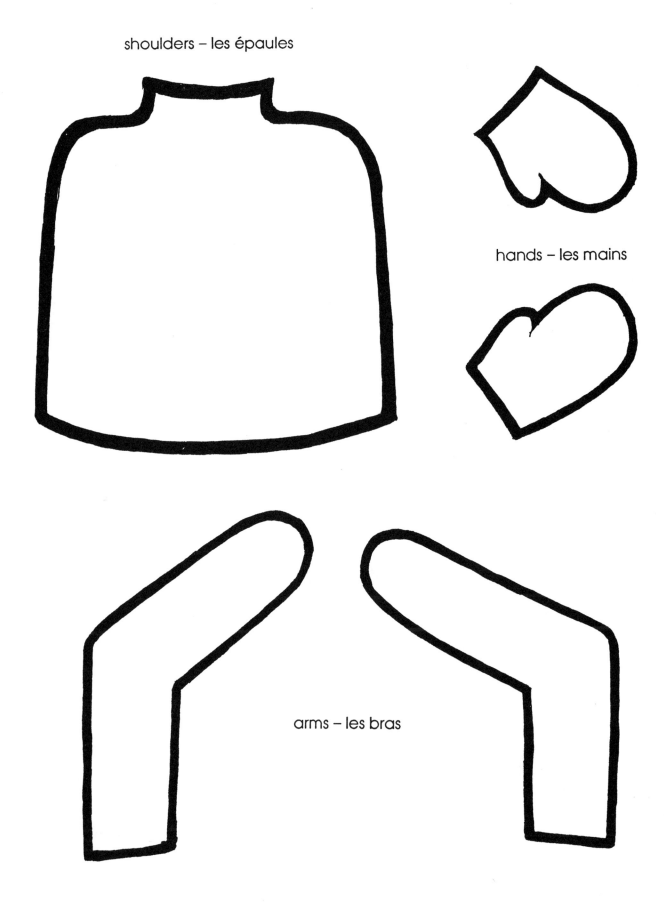

hands – les mains

arms – les bras

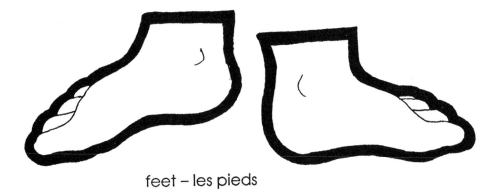

feet – les pieds

legs – les jambes

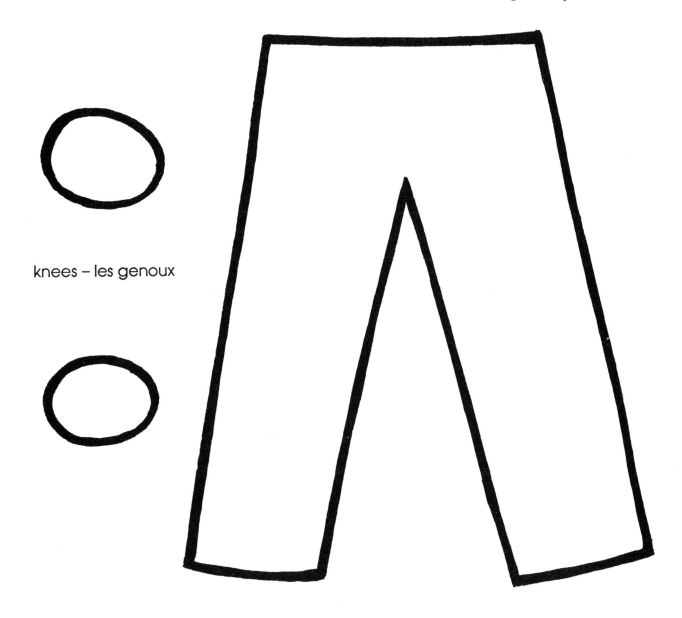

knees – les genoux

SPIN DIAL GAME

Use the pattern below to make a spin dial. Use a brad to attach the arrow. To make the dial more sturdy the pattern could be attached to a heavier cardboard stock and/or laminated. Then, cut out the flashcards for the appropriate unit of body parts. Have children take turns spinning the dial and choosing a flash card. Children should make up an action corresponding to their French body part flashcard and repeat it as many times as the dial indicates.

Example: A child chooses "la tête" for the French vocabulary word and spins the number 3 on the spin dial. The child might tell the other children to touch their head three times, or roll their heads three times.

Note: As children become familiar with their French numbers they can call out the number they spin in French.

MY FRENCH PUPPET

Reproduce this page for each child in your class. Have the children color and cut out the puppet parts. Attach with brads. Let the puppets tell you the names of all it's body parts in French.

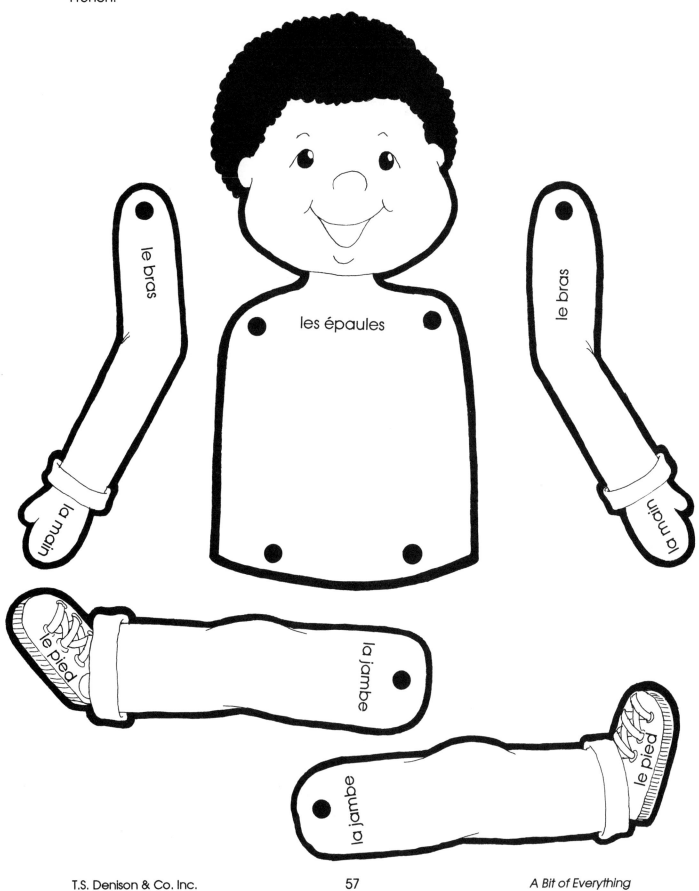

BODY PARTS

FUN SHEET

When the children appear to have a solid comprehension of the new vocabulary in the "Parts of the Body" unit, have them color the picture below to place in their French workbook.

I KNOW MY BODY PARTS IN FRENCH

DATE _____

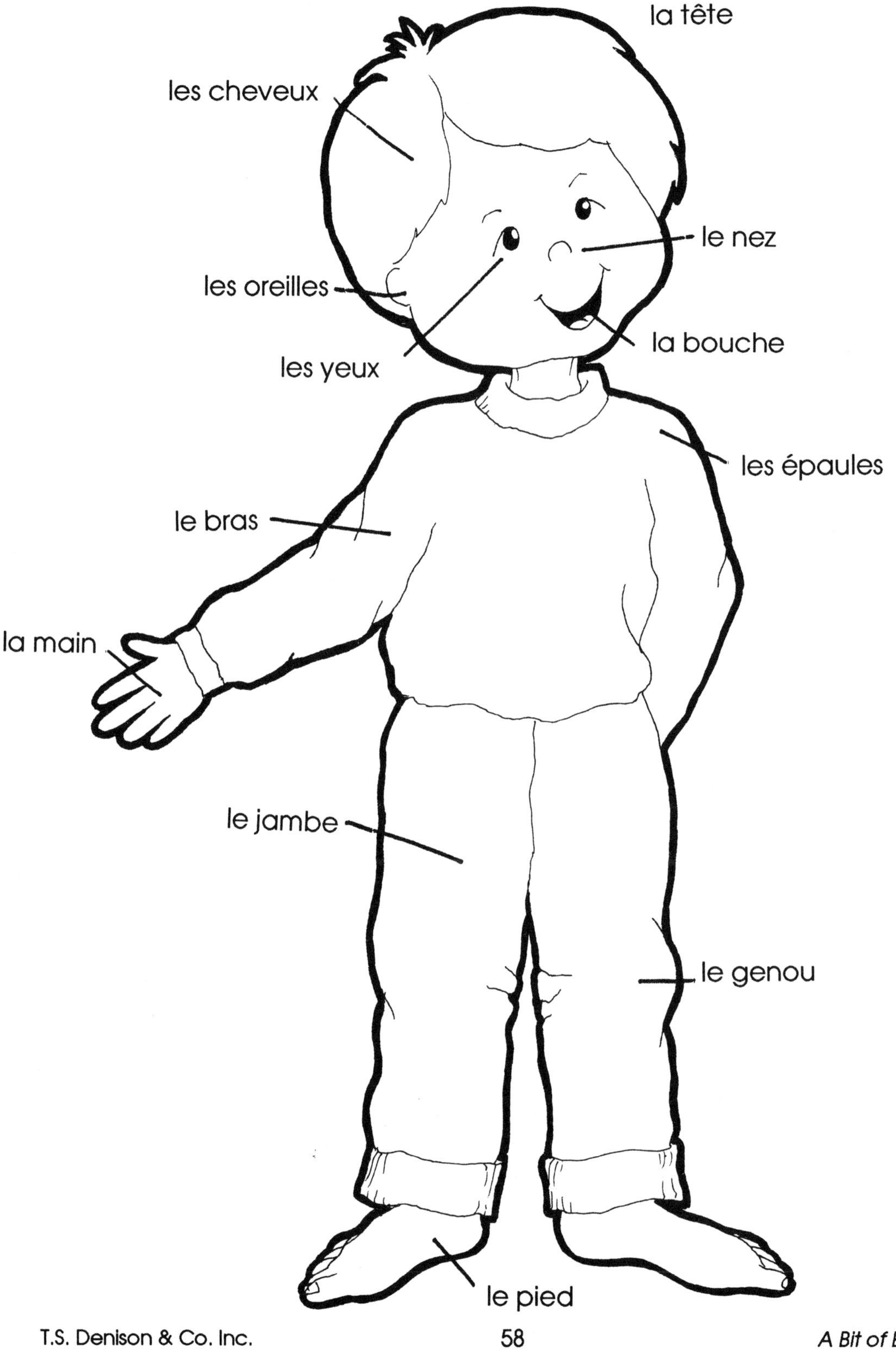

la tête

les cheveux

le nez

les oreilles

la bouche

les yeux

les épaules

le bras

la main

le jambe

le genou

le pied

les oreilles	la bouche
le nez	les yeux
les épaules	les bras
les mains	les jambes
les genoux	les pieds

mouth	**ears**
eyes	**nose**
arms	**shoulders**
legs	**hands**
feet	**knees**

UNIT 7

ARTICLES OF CLOTHING

VOCABULARY

		(pronunciation)
shirt	la chemise	la shuh-meez
pants	le pantalon	luh pahn-tah-lohn
dress	la robe	lah rohb
shorts	le short	luh shorh
sweater	le pull	luh pōōl
socks	les chaussettes	lay shoh-seht
shoes	les chaussures	lay shoh-sewr
hat	le chapeau	luh shah-po
jacket	la veste	lah vest
tie	la cravate	lah krah-vaht

FELT BOARD DRESS UP PATTERNS

Learning the French vocabulary for articles of clothing comes naturally when it is a daily routine topic. The following three pages will provide you with the clothing patterns and the girl and boy felt board characters. Leave the characters and the clothing options up on a felt board and allow students to dress them on their own. Be certain that students are first introduced to the French vocabulary for this unit and that they remember to use it when they are playing with the girl and boy cut-outs during their free time. These patterns can also be used for group activities. Children can take turns dressing the character cut-outs while reciting his articles of clothing in French! *(Let the children in your class give the characters French names.)*

shirt
la chemise

jacket
la veste

shoes
les chaussures

socks
les chaussettes

FELT BOARD DRESS UP PATTERNS

hat
le chapeau

sweater
le pull

pant
le pantalon

dress
la robe

tie
la cravate

shorts
le short

GIRL AND BOY DRESS-UP CHARACTERS

DRESS UP BOX

The ever-popular dress up box in your class can become a completely new and exciting experience for your students. Add some new clothing to the box and label it with the new French vocabulary. Then allow children to use the articles of clothing as they would on any other given day, but require that they use their new French vocabulary while they role play.

"MADAME MAY I"

Many people remember the familiar game "Mother May I?" This game is quite similar and is a great tool to ingrain the new vocabulary for this unit. Choose one child to be the "Madame." Have all the other children line up across the room facing the Madame. The Madame must face away from the children. While doing this the children quietly ask if they may take a certain number of steps forwards. "Madame" can not look at the children but can respond by saying a "If you are wearing a _____ then you may take _____ steps forward." The blanks must be filled with a French vocabulary word for a particular article of clothing and a randomly chosen number of steps for the classmate(s) to take forward – in French, of course! Those children wearing that article called out by the "Madame" may move forward the number of steps indicated. The first child to reach the "Madame" may assume her/his role as the Madame (or Monsieur if the child is a male).

Color the articles of clothing below. Then with a friend, discuss when you would wear each particular article of clothing. Remember to only use your French vocabulary. If you can recall vocabulary from other units try to use it as well.

shoes
les chaussures

hat
le chapeau

sweater
le pull

dress
la robe

shirt
la chemise

socks
les chaussettes

jacket
la veste

tie
la cravate

pant
le pantalon

shorts
le short

la chemise	**les chaussettes**
le pantalon	**la robe**
le chapeau	**les chaussures**
le short	**le pull**
la veste	**la cravate**

Unit 7 Vocabulary – Articles of Clothing

socks

shirt

dress

pants

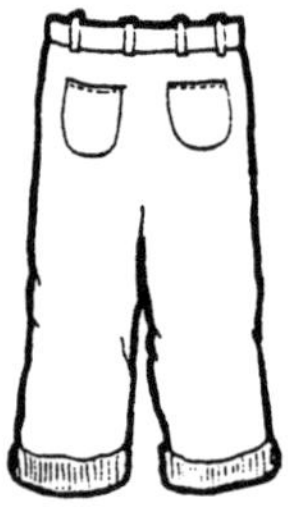

shoes

hat

sweater

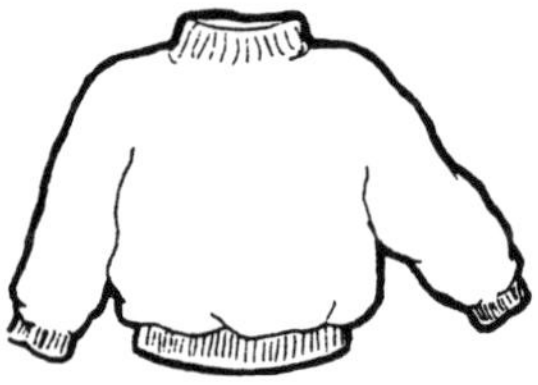

shorts

tie

jacket

UNIT 8

FOODS

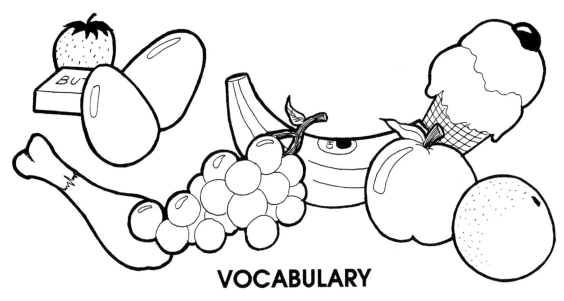

VOCABULARY

		(pronunciation)
milk	le lait	*luh lay*
water	l' eau	*low*
bread	le pain	*luh pahn*
ice cream	la glace	*lah glahss*
grapes	les raisins	*lay ray-zan*
apple	la pomme	*lah pohm*
orange	l' orange	*loh-rahnzh*
banana	la banane	*lah bah-nahn*
cake	le gâteau	*luh gah-toh*
butter	le beurre	*luh buhr*
egg	l' oeuf	*luhf*
chicken	le poulet	*luh poo-leh*
cereal	les céréales	*lay sehr-ay-ell*
salad	la salade	*lah sa-lahd*
hamburger	le hamburger	*luh ah<u>m</u>-boor-gher*
chocolate	le chocolat	*luh shoh-koh-lah*
candy	les bonbons	*lay bohn bohn*
strawberry	la fraise	*lah frehz*
potato	la pomme de terre	*lah pohm duh tehr*
carrot	la carotte	*lah kah-roht*

FOOD PATTERNS

Use the cut out patterns from page 70 through 72 to make replicas of favorite foods. These patterns can be used for felt boards, or can be cut out of a heavier card stock for game use.

bread
le pain

hamburger
le hamburger

carrot
la carotte

chocolate
le chocolot

potato
la pomme de terre

candy
les bonbons

FOOD PATTERNS

cake
le gâteau

cereal
les céréales

open here

LAIT

MILK

milk
le lait

water
l' eau

banana
la banane

salad
la salade

grapes
les raisins

FOOD PATTERNS

strawberry
la fraise

chicken
le poulet

ice cream
la glace

orange
l' orange

butter
le beurre

egg
l' oeuf

apple
la pomme

FRENCH MENU GAMES

Using the food patterns from the previous pages, have the children design menus for a French restaurant. They must put all the names of the food on the menu (younger children could draw pictures instead of writing the words). When the menus have been designed, set up a role play stage. For the first time, set up a table with place settings for four people. Then choose four children who have confidence with their new French vocabulary. Have one person be the waiter/waitress who takes the orders. Orders must be placed using the French food vocabulary.

FRENCH LUNCH DAY

Have all the children bring a lunch to school. Set up a picnic environment in the classroom or outdoors. Have each child take turns telling what they have in their lunch using as much of their French food vocabulary as possible. A French dictionary may be very helpful to you! Children will likely ask if you know vocabulary for other items in their lunches. Manger Bien (Eat Well)!

A FRENCH FAVORITE

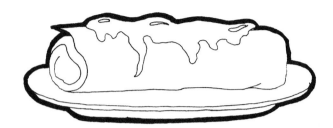

Crepe ingredients:

1 1/2 cups milk
1 1/2 cups flour
3 eggs
1/4 teaspoon salt
2 tablespoons butter or margarine, melted

Combine all ingredients in a mixer or blender until smooth. Let the batter sit for one hour before beginning to bake. Slowly heat a lightly greased 8 inch skillet. Pour 1/4 of a cup of the batter into the center of the pan. Tilt the skillet quickly so that the batter spreads evenly over the pan. Use a spatula to lift the crepe from the skillet. Put the crepes on a plate. Continue to stack them and keep them covered with a towel. If you desire they can be cooked in advance and refrigerated until use.

When ready to serve, pick your favorite topping. French people eat crepes for any meal or dessert. Most children enjoy the dessert variety! Pick a favorite fruit topping, honey, or syrup. If you really want a treat, place a dab of whipped creme on the top!

FOOD BINGO GAME

Copy the cards provided to make enough copies so that each child in the class has at least one card. Use whatever markers you have available (dots, beans, popcorn kernels, etc.). Place the cut-out patterns from the first page of this unit in a bag. Then draw the food from the bag to start the game. The first child to cover a line of three wins the game. Remember to use only French vocabulary for the foods. Allow different children the opportunity to draw the food cards from the bag.

FOOD BINGO

FOOD BINGO

FOOD BINGO

FOOD BINGO

PREPARE A MEAL

Have the children cut out pictures of food from magazines. Ask the children to plan a meal using the pictures of food they have found. Glue the pictures on the plate. Can the children name the foods using their French vocabulary?

FOOD COLORING

Color all the foods that you can remember from the French Food Unit. If there **FUN SHEET**
is a food you have forgotten, ask a friend for help.

le lait	les raisins
l' eau	la pomme
l' orange	le pain
le gâteau	la glace
le beurre	l'oeuf

Unit 8 Vocabulary – Foods

grapes

milk

apple

water

bread

orange

ice cream

cake

egg

butter

le poulet	les céréales
la salade	la banane
la fraise	la carotte
le hamburger	le chocolat
les bonbons	la pomme de terre

Unit 8 Vocabulary – Foods

cereal

chicken

banana

salad

carrot

strawberry

chocolate

hamburger

potato

candy

UNIT 9
ANIMALS

VOCABULARY

		(pronunciation)
cat	le chat	*luh shah*
dog	le chien	*luh she-eh*
cow	la vache	*lah vahsh*
horse	le cheval	*luh-sha-vahl*
chicken	le poulet	*luh-poo-leh*
pig	le cochon	*luh kush-oh*
sheep	le mouton	*luh moo-tohn*
bird	l' oiseau	*lehwa-zoh*
bear	l' ours	*lehoors*
snake	le serpent	*luh sehr-pahn*

ANIMAL PATTERNS

Patterns for cut-outs of animals are found on pages 84 & 85. Each animal is labeled with the appropriate French vocabulary. Introduce the children to the new vocabulary and arrange the animals for a bulletin board display.

bird
l' oiseau

sheep
le mouton

chicken
le poulet

cow
la vache

snake
le serpent

ANIMAL PATTERNS

cat
le chat

bear
l' ours

pig
le cochon

dog
le chien

horse
le cheval

WHO'S ZOO?

Have each child bring a stuffed animal from home. Designate a corner of your room for the *Who's Zoo*. Have each child display their stuffed animal in that corner. Have each child introduce their animal using first the English name they chose for their pretend pet, and then what type of animal it is using the new French vocabulary word. (Example: "Hi, this is Fluffy. He is un *chien*.")

ANIMAL SOUNDS

Old MacDonald is an all-time favorite song that can be used for reinforcing the French vocabulary for different animals. Try the combinations below using the old familiar tune.

And on his farm he had . . . a un chien   with a . . . bark, bark, here
un chat   meow, meow, here
un cheval   nah, nah, here
une vache   moo, moo, here
un serpent   sss, sss, here

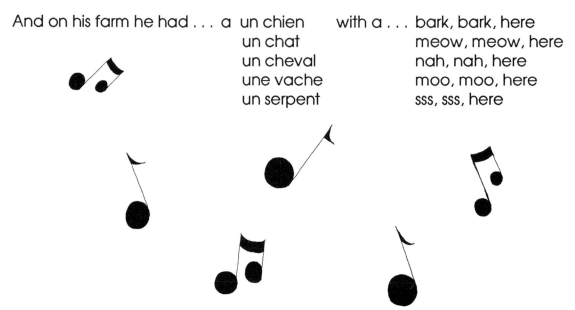

ANIMAL PUPPETS

Give each of the children a lunch-size paper bag, construction paper and a variety of different colored scrap paper. Using the paper, let the children create a paper bag puppet. Each child should know the animal's name in French. When the puppets are complete, let the children put on a puppet show with their French animal. It is also fun to sing *Old MacDonald Had A Farm,* singing the animal's names in French.

ANIMAL MATCHING

FUN SHEET

Draw a line from the adult animal on the left to the baby animal on the right.
Can you say the name of the animal in French?

le chat	**le chien**
le poulet	**le serpent**
le cheval	**la vache**
l' ours	**le cochon**
l' oiseau	**le mouton**

Unit 9 Vocabulary – Animals

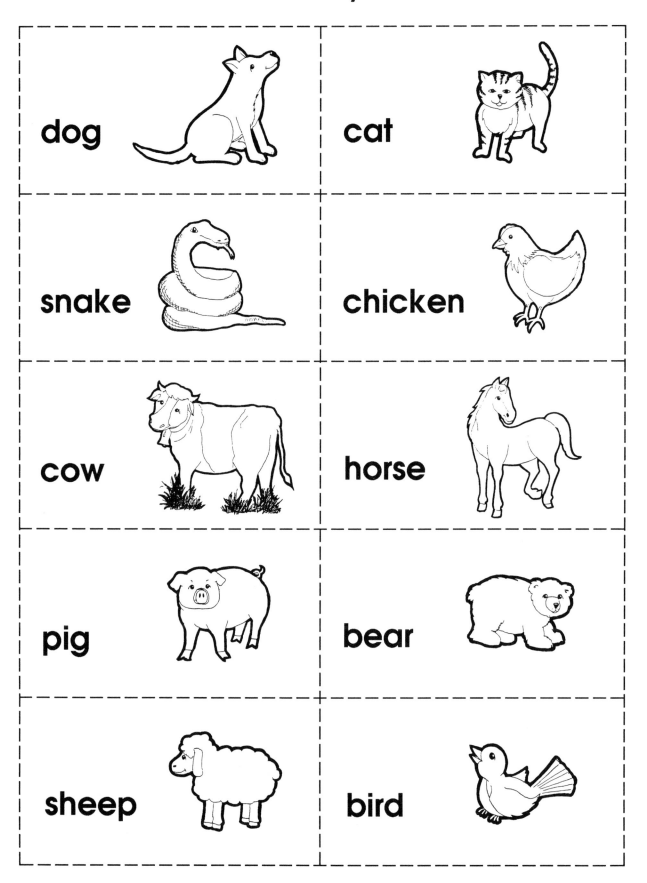

dog

cat

snake

chicken

cow

horse

pig

bear

sheep

bird

UNIT 10
FAMILY MEMBERS

VOCABULARY

		(pronunciation)
mother	la mère	*lah mehr*
father	le père	*luh pehr*
sister	la soeur	*lah suhr*
brother	le frère	*luh frehr*
grandmother	la grand-mère	*lah grah-mehr*
grandfather	le grand-père	*luh grah-pehr*
aunt	la tante	*lah t' ahnt*
uncle	l'oncle	*lohn-clah*
cousin	*(masculine)* le cousin	*luh coo-zan*
	(femine) la cousine	*lah coo-zine*
cat	le chat	*luh shah*
dog	le chien	*luh she-eh*
baby	le bébé	*luh beh beh*

PATTERNS FOR FAMILY MEMBERS

Use the patterns below and on page 93 for cut outs to introduce the new "family members" vocabulary. Allow children to arrange them on either a felt board or bulletin board. Remember to keep the display boards at a level low enough so that the children can French role play on their own.

baby
le bébé

sister
la soeur

grandmother
la grand-mère

grandfather
le grand-père

PATTERNS FOR FAMILY MEMBERS

brother
le frère

father
le père

mother
la mère

STORY TIME

Read a familiar story like, "The Three Bears," using the French vocabulary for the family members. Then have the children retell the story from memory using the new vocabulary and any other unit vocabulary they may recall. Storytime might easily become a language experience as well. On a large piece of paper, use bold print to write the story being retold by the children. Highlight the new French vocabulary using a different colored marker. Finally, after the story is complete, have the children assist you in rereading what you have written.

PICTURE DAY

Have each child bring a picture of his/her family. Encourage the children to bring a photograph that includes their extended family if possible. Have each child take a turn showing their photograph and introducing the members of their family using the vocabulary from this unit. As an extension to this activity, make a bulletin board display that is in the form of a tree. Stick each child's photograph on the tree and label the pictures with child's first name (Erick's family, etc.).

Color the people below. Draw a line to match the picture with the French word for the person.

la mère

le frère

le père

la soeur

le bébé

la mère	le père
la grand-mère	le grand-père
la soeur	le frère
la tante	l' oncle
le cousin la cousine	le bébé

father	**mother**
grandfather	**grandmother**
brother	**sister**
uncle	**aunt**
baby	**cousin**

UNIT 11

MODES OF TRANSPORTATION

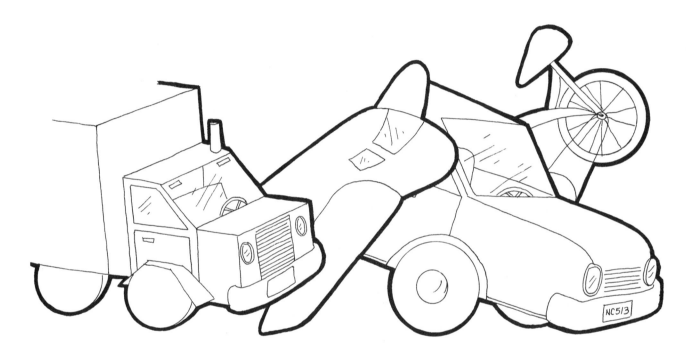

VOCABULARY

		(pronunciation)
car	la voiture	lah vwah-tewr
bus	l' autobus	loh-toh-bewss
truck	le camion	luh kah-mee-ohn
bike	le vélo	luh veh-loh
boat	le bateau	luh bah-toh
plane	l' avion	lah-vee-ohn
ski	le ski	luh skee
helicopter	le hélicoptere	luh eh-lee-kohpt-ehr
air balloon	le ballon aérostat	luh bah-loh nahy-roh-stah
scooter	la trotinette	lah troht-in-ehette

MODES OF TRANSPORTATION

Collect a large box of magazines. Have children cut out pictures which show various modes of transportation (remember to define "transportation" to the younger children). Then have the children glue the pictures on a large board in collage form. When the collage is complete, have a group discussion and introduce the children to the vocabulary for modes of transportation. Display the collage in the classroom for the remainder of the unit.

INDEPENDENTLY CREATIVE TRANSPORTATION

Give the children a period of uninterrupted time to use legos or building blocks of some sort to build a vehicle. Try to keep the children working independently or in very small groups, this will encourage individual creativity. Finally, allow children to share their masterpieces in front of the class. Remember to have children use their French vocabulary in their introductions.

FUN SHEET

Color the picture of the different forms of transportation below. Practice the new vocabulary before finding a friend to review the words. After reviewing the words, take turns telling your friend how you would use each mode of transportation. For example: " I would use *le bateau* to travel over water or go water skiing."

scooter
la trotinette

bike
le vélo

plane
l' avion

truck
le camion

car
la voiture

boat
le bateau

bus
l' autobus

helicopter
l'helicoptère

ski
le ski

air balloon
le ballon aérostat

l' avion	l' autobus
la voiture	le bateau
le vélo	le camion
la trotinette	le ski
l'helicoptère	le ballon aérostat

Unit 11 Vocabulary – Modes of Transportation

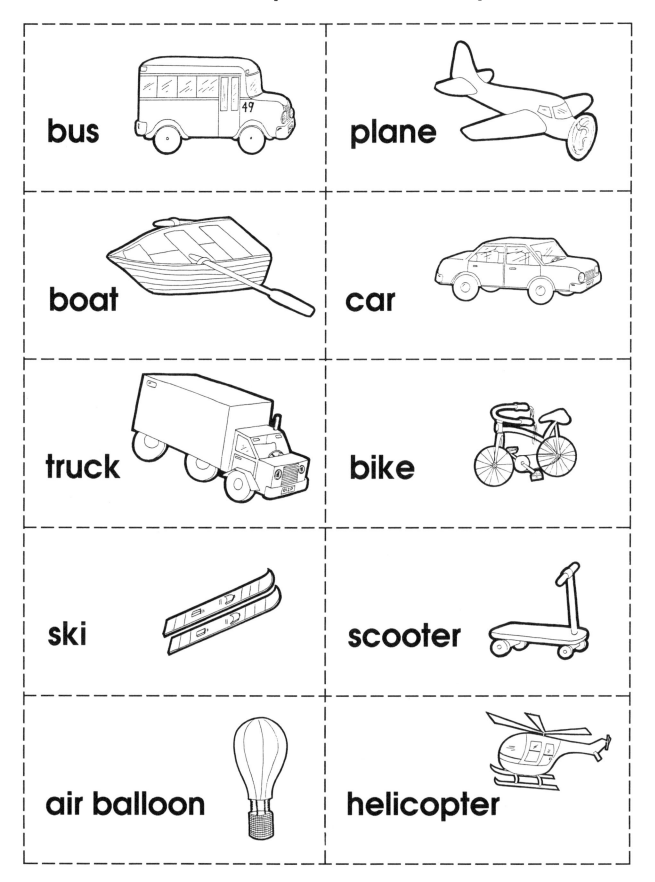

bus

plane

boat

car

truck

bike

ski

scooter

air balloon

helicopter

UNIT 12

SPECIAL PLACES

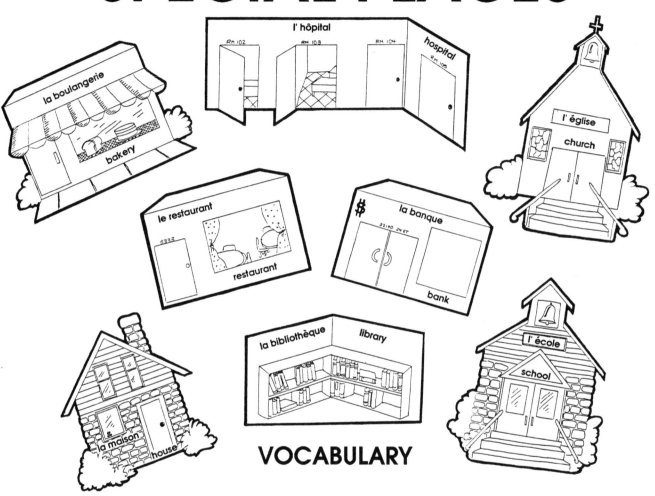

VOCABULARY

		(pronunciation)
house	la maison	*la meh-zhon*
kitchen	la cusine	*lah kwee-zeen*
bedroom	la chambre á coucher	*lah shahm-bruh ah koo-shay*
school	l' école	*lay-kohl*
library	la bibliothèque	*lah bee-blee-oh-tehk*
hospital	l' hôpital	*loh-pee-tahl*
church	l' église	*lay-gleez*
restaurant	le restaurant	*luh rehss-toh-rahn*
bakery	la boulangerie	*lah boo-lahn-zhree*
bank	la banque	*lah bahnk*

SPECIAL PLACES

Introduce your class to two new vocabulary words each day by simulating two different role play areas in your classroom. Some of the places will need little or no effort to establish (like the role play area for the word "school"). Divide the class in half and allow the children to have free time playing in each area. Do this for 15 minutes a day for one week to reinforce the new vocabulary.

SPECIAL PLACES MATCHING GAME PATTERNS

Copy the patterns on pages 106 through 109. Have children match the objects with the room or place to which it belongs. For example: "The book comes from the bibliothèque." Allow the children to lead the group, reminding them to only use the new French vocabulary from this unit.

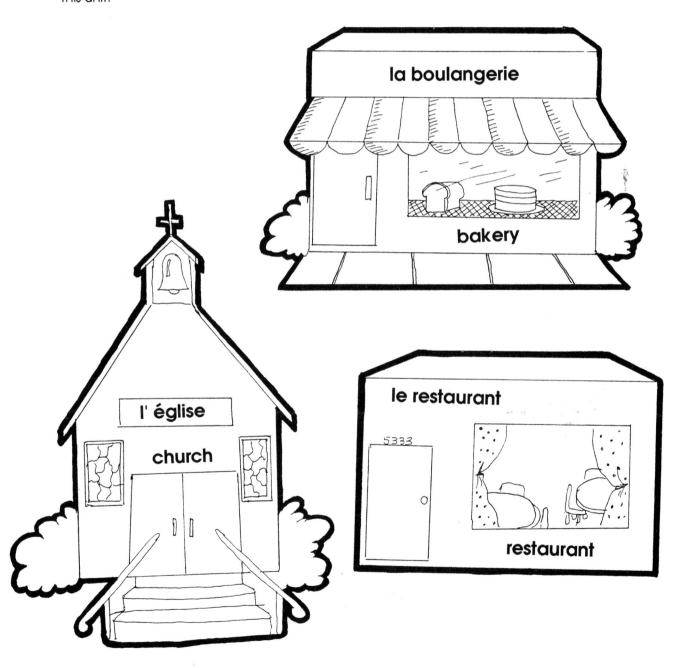

SPECIAL PLACES MATCHING GAME PATTERNS

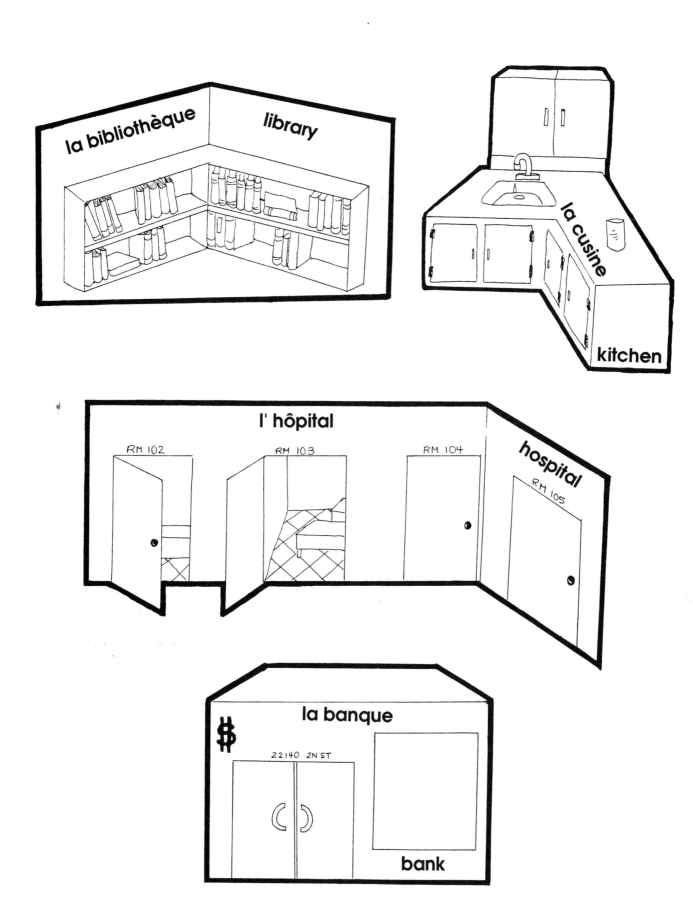

la bibliothèque   library

la cusine   kitchen

l' hôpital   hospital

RM 102   RM 103   RM 104   RM 105

la banque   bank

$

22140 2N ST

SPECIAL PLACES MATCHING GAME PATTERNS

bedroom

la chambre á coucher

l' école

school

la maison

house

SPECIAL PLACES MATCHING GAME PATTERNS

SPECIAL PLACES

FUN SHEET

Look at each of the special places. Draw a picture of something that you would find at that special place.

house la maison	kitchen la cusine	bedroom la chambre á coucher
school l' école	library la bibliothèque	hospital l' hôpital
restaurant le restaurant	bakery la boulangerie	bank la banque

la maison	**l' hôpital**
la cuisine	**l' église**
la chambre á coucher	**le restaurant**
l' école	**la boulangerie**
la bibliothèque	**la banque**

Unit 12 Vocabulary – Special Places

hospital

house

church

kitchen

restaurant

bedroom

bakery

school

bank

library

UNIT 13

COMMON PHRASES

VOCABULARY

		(pronunciation)
Hello	Bonjour	bohn-zhoor
How are you?	Ça va?	sah vah?
Things are going fine	Oui ça va.	wee sahva
And you?	Et toi?	eh twah?
Very well	Très bien	treh-b' yan
Thank you	Merci	mehr-ssee
What time is it?	Quelle heure est-il?	kehl uhr eh-teel?
It is ___ o'clock	Il est ___ heure.	eel eh ___ uhr.
Good-bye	Au revoir	oh-ruh-vwahr
Good night	Bonsoir	bohn-swahr

COMMON PHRASES

By making it a routine to begin each French group time using the same greetings, your students will quickly acquire some common French phrases into their vocabulary. Begin by writing down the greetings on a large piece of paper. Have students follow along with the readings for the first couple weeks and slowly remove or cover a portion of the text until all can be recited from memory. Use the paragraph below as a guideline to transfer the phrases to a large poster-sized board.

Reader: Bonjour! Ça va?
Students: Oui, ça va! Et toi?
Reader: Très bien, merci.
Students: Quelle heure est-il?
Reader: Il est ___ heure.
Students: Merci et au revoir.
Reader: Bonsoir!

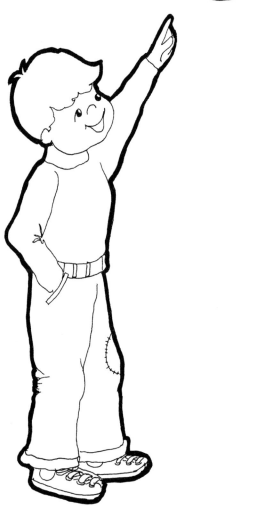

Bonjour	**Quelle heure est-il?**
Ça va?	**Il est ___ heure.**
Très bien	**Merci**
Et toi?	**Au revoir**
Bonsoir	**Oui ça va**

What time is it?	**Hello**
It is ___ o'clock	**How are you?**
Thank you	**Very well**
Good-bye	**And you?**
Things are going fine	**Good night**

THE FRENCH FLAG

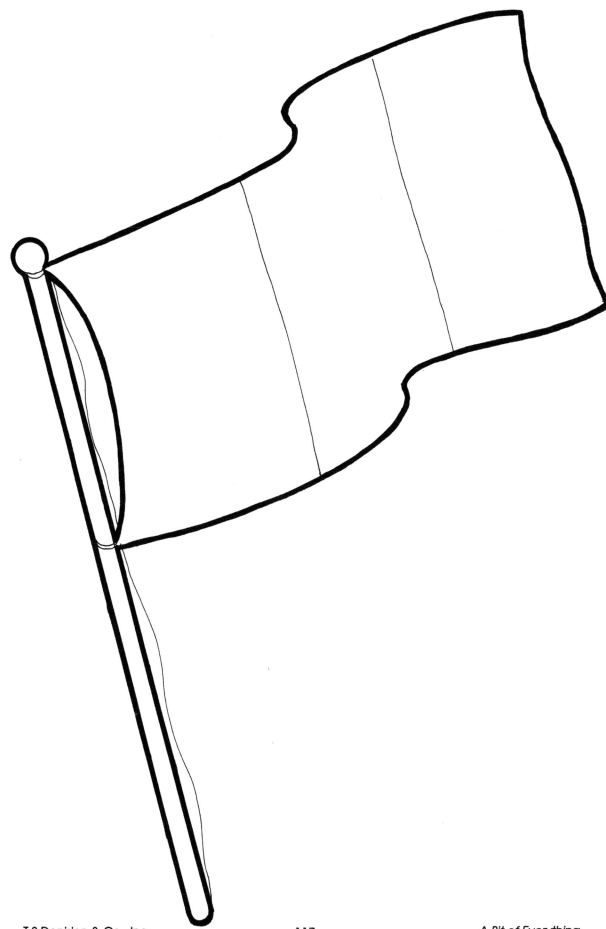

THE CANADIAN FLAG

MAP OF FRANCE

Draw in some of the things that you think you might see in France.

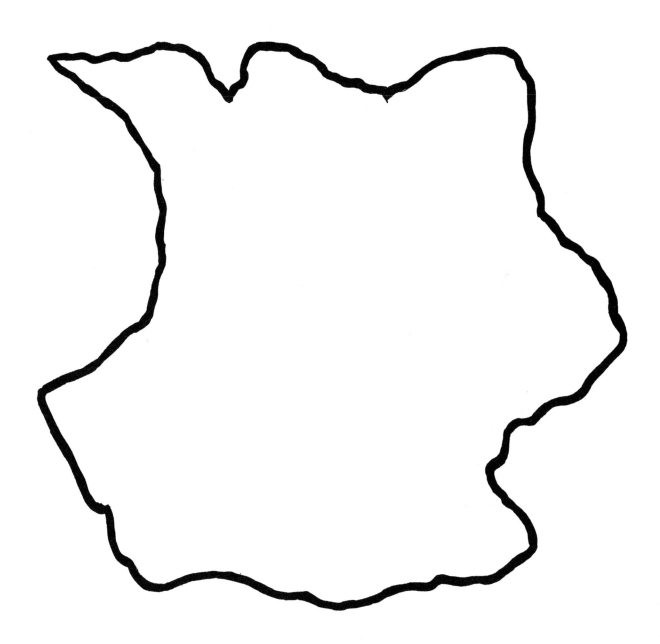

MAP OF CANADA

Draw in some of the things that you think you might see in Canada.